The Kennedys

JFK and Jackie Kennedy
2 Books in 1

Phil Coleman and Katy Holborn

Table of Contents

INSIDE CAMELOT

The True Story of the Assassination
of JFK (Conspiracy Theories Book 1)

Phil Coleman

Introduction

John F. Kennedy was elected as the 35th president of the United States in 1960. At that time, he was a member of one of the wealthiest families in America. He had an extremely elite education and was considered a military hero, though his act of heroism is still questioned by many.

His running mate for the election was not his to choose and was not someone he cared to have as a vice-president. Lyndon B. Johnson was not a personable man, he lacked charm, and thought he, himself was handsome and funny. Neither of which were true. Lyndon had been put in place as his running mate by the political machine and Lyndon hated the Kennedy's.

John Fitzegerald Kennedy did win the race, but not without the help of his father who had connections with organized crime. Joe Kennedy had asked that the crime bosses stuff the ballot boxes which was easy to do in 1960, and if they did that John F. Kennedy would leave organized crime alone while he was in office. John F. Kennedy did leave organized crime alone, but not Bobby Kennedy. Bobby went after them with a vengeance. When the popular votes were counted, Kennedy had won by only a little over 100,000 of the popular votes of over 68 million votes cast. Of course, when the Electoral College votes were added up, Kennedy had clearly won.

Inside Camelot

As discussed in the introduction, John F. Kennedy was in PT-109 while in service when a Japanese destroyer hit his boat with him and all his men on board, virtually cutting their boat in half. Members of the crew on the destroyer felt that it was no accident, others act as though the captain acted like he never realized what had happened.

Seamen Marney and Kirksey were lost, as well as two other crew members who were seriously injured. Being such a catastrophic collision, followed by an explosion and a fire, their loss rate was low compared to others who had suffered the same fate. The PT-109 kept the forward hull floating in a virtual sea of flames.

PT-169 sent out two torpedoes that had missed the destroyer and PT-162's torpedoes did not fire at all. Both boats left the scene of action and went back to base without checking on any survivors.

Despite being injured himself, Kennedy towed Patrick McMahon on shore by holding a strap from McMahon's life jacket between his teeth. It was not until six days later that native islanders noticed them and went for help. They were rescued the next day. Jack's brother, not so lucky. He died a year later as his plane was blown up in Europe during a dangerous mission.

Kennedy was not a well man, and his health records document this. These records were kept highly confidential for years, but have finally come to light in 2008.

He suffered from colon, prostate problems, high fevers, stomach, dehydration, sleeplessness, high cholesterol, and he had so much going on with his back and adrenal problems.

He had to be prescribed medications like Lomotil, paregoric, Metamucil, testosterone, phenobarbital, and trasentine to control his diarrhea, weight loss, penicillin, and abdominal discomfort and other antibiotics for his urinary tract infections and an abscess; he had to take Tuinal so he could sleep. Before he would have a press, conference or hold any type of televised speech, his doctors would increase his cortisone dose so he could better deal with tension harmful to someone not able to produce his own corticosteroids.

John met Jackie at a dinner party. She said he had leaned across the table where the asparagus was at and asked her out on a date. One year later, September 12, 1953, they were husband and wife. They were a beautiful couple indeed.

John and Jackie Kennedy's marriage has always been referred to as Camelot. Jackie made that up when her children were little. She wanted their family and their home and the white house to sound like they were living a fairy tale to children Jack Jr. and Caroline.

John F. Kennedy was the charming prince and Jackie the fair princess; both in their white castle. The couple that everyone else in the world wanted their life and marriage to be like. The marriage truly seemed like the magic from which fairytales were made.

But, as we know, life is not always as it seems. Unfortunately, John F. Kennedy seemed to 'like' all women, too much as a matter of fact. So much so, that his brother Robert always had to come behind him and clean up his "messes" to make him look like the fairy tale prince to his ever adoring public.

There were the rumors, and there were a lot of them. The rumors about Marilyn Monroe seemed to all be true. When you research the facts, some say that Jack enjoyed the company of men more than women and that he got the women to come in for his brother, but he made it look like it was for him. Jack, it is said, had interest in only one man. This has never been a proven fact, but there were many rumors running rampant at the time.

There were rumors about him and his gay friend, Lem from boarding school at Choate. Though being gay was not talked about in the 1960's; Lem was gay and he stayed at the White House a lot while Jack was president. He one time said that Jack kept him from being so lonely and that John F. Kennedy was probably why he never got married.

Did Jackie know about the other women in her husband's life? Yes, unfortunately she did. And, it hurt her to the core. Did she ever quit loving him? It doesn't appear that she ever did. Even on the day that he was killed, she still loved him and was a devoted wife.

Some say this all happened a long time ago, and it did. Some say, that since it did happen a long time ago, it does not matter and that no one cares. Not true. What happened on that fateful day in November 1963 in Dallas, Texas affected the entire world and changed the course of political history forever. Everyone should care.

Jackie Kennedy was brought up to be a lady. She was the perfect first lady for the white house, unmatched by any other since that time. She knew how to dress fashionably, she knew how to entertain distinguished guests from all over the world and make them feel comfortable. She was matched perfectly for her role in the White House.

Jack Kennedy's first three years in office were not easy. He met with many challenges and they were tough challenges upon which to be re-elected and the type to make enemies. His failure with the "Bay of Pigs" in Cuba. The Cuban Missile crisis came so near to bringing us to nuclear war that U.S. citizens still talk about it today.

The CIA's reputation was tarnished from the failed 'Bay of Pigs' mission and John F.

Kennedy replaced Allen W. Dulles as head of the CIA.

John F. Kennedy never brought troops home from Vietnam, he just kept sending more. It felt to America that the war in Vietnam would never come to an end.   It was like a gigantic black hole that money and U.S. soldiers were being thrown into and covered up.

On November 22nd, 1963 in Dallas, Texas as Governor John Connelly and his wife were in the front seat of the open top convertible and Jack and Jackie Kennedy in the back seat smiling and waving at the crowd of onlookers. The parade route took them right in front of the Book Depository Building for Texas Schools, and someone fired shots, killing President Kennedy and injuring Governor Connelly seriously.

They were rushed immediately to Dallas' Parkland Hospital. There was absolutely no chance for President Kennedy, the shots had hit him in the skull shattering it wide open and what it contained spewed everywhere into the air and in the car. Jackie was beside herself as she held her husband's head in her lap; still thinking that maybe they could help him, but knowing deep down inside, her Camelot had just come to a terrible end.

Jackie could not be consoled. She did not want to leave her husband's body when they put it in the cargo hold of the plane later that day. She refused to change her blood-soaked clothes. She wanted the world to see what they had done to their President.

As an aside note; Jackie never got rid of this suit. It is today, in the National Archives Building in Maryland. It came with a note from Jackie's mother. The suit has never been cleaned and it never will be.

In 2003 Caroline Kennedy gave this suit to the people of the United States. She gave instructions that it could not be placed on display until 2103. Instructions are that before it can be placed on display; the Kennedy's must be consulted.

The pill box hat Jackie wore that day has forever disappeared. The Secret Service got their hands on it and that was the last anyone has ever seen of it.

Johnson however, could not wait to be President and insisted he be sworn in aboard Airforce One before they took off for the return trip back to Washington D.C. with John F. Kennedy's body.

He was in such a hurry to take the oath of office, that he called Jack's grieving brother, Bobby Kennedy and asked him to get the wording for him so they could take care of the swearing in immediately.

On Monday after the assassination, a horse drawn carriage bore John Fitzgerald Kennedy's body from the Capitol Rotunda to St. Matthew's Catholic Church for mass.

From there it went on to Arlington National Cemetery where he was laid to rest and an eternal flame was lit to mark his grave for the entire world to see.

Political Insiders Involved

As with all things good or bad, years later people have come and gone, more things come to light, and so they have. Deathbed confessions, prisoners telling other prisoners, and eventually the pieces all fall into place.

It started with a group that wanted to take the government into their own hands and get rid of the policies that Kennedy had put into place. He was never supposed to have won. In their minds, he had screwed everything up that they had planned.

This group all found themselves in bed together and had been there for some time before that fateful day in November 1963. Governor Connelly even knew what was going to go down that horrible day.

He had supposedly been the one who had marked out the parade route. The parade route that was changed from what the secret service had planned. Connally was an ally of Johnson's. In fact, he had lost the fight over seating arrangements for the motorcade and was 'forced' to ride with John F. Kennedy and Jackie.

At the highest level of conspiracy, you have Lyndon Johnson, George Herbert Walker Bush, Richard Nixon, Gerald Ford, J. Edgar Hoover, and Prescott Bush.

There was a man by the name of Morales, who had evolved in the CIA as their best assassin from Latin America. He became very close to David Atlee Phillips and he happened to be the Chief of Operations at the CIA in Miami. Here is where they would train Cuban exiles and prepare them for raids against Castro.

The head of that station was Ted Shackley. He was an associate of George Herbert Walker Bush. You will realize the connection when Bush is appointed CIA director and then appoints his friend Shackley as his Deputy Director.

There was an oil geologist by the name of George Demohrenschildt, that knew all the oil barons in Texas and this included all the

Bush family. It was felt that the oil geologist was also managing Oswald and building him up to think he was going to be a hero.

He had worked with Oswald and made him think that he was going to infiltrate and stop an assassination plot.

George Herbert Walker Bush lied by saying he had nothing to do with the CIA in 1963. There is a document however, that is written by J. Edgar Hoover himself that proves he was in contact with George Herbert Walker Bush about the John F. Kennedy assassination specifically with Hoover, and his concern about how the Cuban exiles would react to this news.

Then there is Richard Nixon, who owed his political career to the Bush family. Prescott Bush had made sure that Nixon was placed on the Republican ticket with Eisenhower as Vice President. At that time, Gerald Ford and George Herbert Walker Bush were fundraisers for the campaign. The Bushes were completely blown over when Kennedy won. They had NO idea that Joe Kennedy had made a deal with the crime boss, Giancana out of Chicago to rig some of the elections.

Let us look closer at Prescott Bush while we are at it. He had made his fortune as a banker and some of it by financing the war effort for none other than Adolf Hitler. Prescott Bush is anything but clean in his dealings as a banker. Of course, you will find his family will do nothing but sing praises of him. Why not? This is where the Bush fortune started.

When Johnson put the Warren Commission into being, who else did he appoint to run it but Gerald Ford and Dulles. Remember, Kennedy had fired Dulles and now Dulles hated the Kennedy's. Gerald Ford hated the Kennedy's and was a big supporter of Richard Nixon and the Bushes.

How could you have a fair investigation into a man's death? The Warren Commission was a complete joke.

It is no secret that Jeb Bush and his family are friends with all the Cuban exiles in Florida. And while Jeb was Governor there, he had their support. No wonder during the 2016 election debates Jeb was so pro-immigrant.

Please bear with me for a moment if I seem to be going too far from 1963. There is logic here, to prove a point.

After 1985, remember the Iran-Contra scandal? It was where weapons were being smuggled to Iran and Nicaragua, and they were being financed supposedly by drug trafficking. Think again. This was led by none other than George Herbert Walker Bush, who was Vice President at the time with Ronald Reagan.

George Herbert Walker Bush used this covert operation to get the American

Hostages released in October by making a deal with the Ayatollah Khomeini. If the Ayatollah would just hold the hostages until they told him to let them go, then the U.S. would give the Ayatollah weapons. That is when Carter lost the election (because Bush had worked to get the hostages released in October before the election) and Reagan and Bush took control.

The list goes on, but a pattern develops that shows the Bushes guiding and protecting assassins and terrorists that helped with killing John F. Kennedy.

It somehow may seem that George Herbert Walker Bush was a puppet master, although behind the scenes he hid. He was a spider hiding in his invisible web of deceit. He was silent but deadly during his time.

Lee Harvey Oswald

Since time has passed and so much has come to light about the assassination, you can almost feel sorry for Oswald. He really was a "Patsy" as he called himself.

Oswald joined the Marines in 1956 and was discharged in 1959. Like every Marine, he had to be tested for his shooting abilities. In December, 1956 he scored 212, barely above the requirements for a sharpshooter. In May, 1959 he scored a 191 and that reduced him to only a marksman.

Oswald found himself court-martialed when he accidentally shot himself in his elbow with a .22 gun he was not permitted to have. If this was not enough, he was court-martialed a second time for fighting with a sergeant that he thought was to blame for his being punished in the shooting matter. It seemed he could not stay out of trouble.

For this, he was demoted from private first class to private and briefly spent some time in the brig. For a third time, while on night-time duty in the Philippines, he for no reason, fired his rifle into the jungle. He was dishonorably discharged from the Marines.

Nine days after discharge he left for the Soviet Union where he tried to become a citizen. When the Marines found out about this they downgraded his discharge even more, to undesirable. Oswald was mad, and for good reason; what he did after he left the

Marines shouldn't have had any bearing on his three years as a Marine.

He married a Soviet woman; they had a daughter and in 1962 returned to the U.S. Oswald decided to try proper channels and sent a heartfelt written plea to Governor Connally. He asked him to re-address what seemed to be a miscarriage of justice that was causing him to not be able to gain decent employment. If Governor Connally could just get his discharge changed to honorable for him, surely, he could find a decent job.

In February, he got a reply; it came in an envelope with Connally's smiling face sticking out through the Texas star. The letter was the usual brush off. He was furious at Connally and blamed him for not being able to get a decent job. Connally could have helped him immensely.

When his wife was interviewed about the assassination, she named Connally as his target. She said he like Kennedy, he even admired John F. Kennedy. He hated Connally and blamed him for all his failures in life when Connally would not help him.

In early 1963 he bought a .38 revolver and a rifle by mail order. April 10th, 1963, he was alleged to have shot at and missed a former U.S. Army General Edwin Walker who was known for his extreme right-wing views. Oswald seemed to bounce everywhere that year, but in October, he came back to Dallas and took a job working at the Book

Depository Building for the Texas School Systems.

Less than one hour after John F. Kennedy was killed, Oswald killed a policeman who had stopped him to ask him some questions near his rooming house. Then he ducked into a movie theater where he thought he could hide out.

He was taken into custody by police shortly after going into the theatre and they locked Oswald into the Dallas jail nearby.

On November 24th, he was being brought into the Dallas police headquarters so he could be taken to a more secure jail. There was a huge crowd gathered and lots of cameras and video equipment. Jack Ruby stepped forward from the crowd, pointed a .38 revolver at Oswald and wounded him. He died shortly thereafter.

A New Orleans District Attorney (who later became a judge) Jim Garrison, in 1967 had brought Clay Shaw to trial finally for his part in the assassination of President Kennedy. Jim's opinion was that Oswald was probably a CIA agent after all, who had been pulled into a plot and was used as a scapegoat.

Around 1978, a former CIA employee who oversaw payroll and accounting by the name of James Willcott testified that Lee Harvey Oswald was in fact a "known agent" of the CIA.

Jack Ruby

When Ruby was asked why he killed Oswald; his reply was because of his outrage for Oswald killing his President. Ruby was charged for first-degree murder. Ruby had to do this, to save his own neck. He had tried another time to kill Oswald, but it had not worked out. He could not fail again.

The officers disarmed, tackled and arrested Ruby and took him to a cell on the fifth floor. He was sweating profusely and acting very hyper. Jack Ruby asked someone for a cigarette. Word eventually came up to his cell that Oswald was dead and one of the detectives told Ruby that it looked like he, Ruby was going to the electric chair.

All at once, Ruby stopped sweating and became very calm. The detective asked him if he needed another cigarette. Ruby told him, not me, I don't even smoke. It became very apparent that Jack Ruby's life depended on whether Oswald died.

Jack Ruby was not new to this scene. He had strip joints and owned dance halls all over Dallas. During this time, Ruby became an informant for the FBI.

Jack Ruby's real name was Jacob Rubenstein. He was a runner for Al Capone at one time. His mob activities stayed with him after he left Chicago and moved to Dallas. Ruby was to be the tie in man. Run criminal activities in Dallas and serve as the liaison to the Chicago Mafia.

When one of Jack Ruby's girls was asked how Oswald and Ruby knew each other, she laughed out loud and said that Ruby's nickname was 'Pinkie', and that Oswald and Ruby had been bed partners for years. How times have changed, today she would have been able to say they were lovers, gay, or life partners. Imagine that, to have to shoot the man who you had shared a bed with all those years to save your own skin.

Apparently, life, no matter in what context, meant nothing in this circle.

Jack Ruby, mob hitman in 1939; CIA in 1950's; FBI informant 1959; meets up with Frank Sturgis and Marita Lorenze to pick up two weapons delivered from Miami, and paid for by cash by E. Howard Hunt on Nov.

21, 1963. Don't forget, Hunt was later convicted in the Watergate mess during Nixon's dirty years.

For some reason, Hunt seems to be everywhere you look. In Texas, in Washington, in Florida, close to Cuba, you name it, you will find Hunt.

Jack Ruby's involvement with the CIA was only for gun smuggling. A young Cuban, Fidel Castro, needed some guns.

The Warren Commission wanted to deny that Ruby had any strong ties or otherwise to the Mafia even with all the overwhelming evidence presented. But, later, a congressional investigation confirmed that he did indeed have ties with the underworld.

In his first trial, the jury sentenced him to death. In October 1966, the Appeals court turned over the decision and while waiting for a new trial, Ruby died of a pulmonary embolism secondary to lung cancer.

Ruby, not too long before his death, had told his psychiatrist that the killing of John/Jack F. Kennedy was "an attempt at overthrowing the U.S. government" and that he himself knew who had killed JFK. He went on to say, that he did not want to die, but he was doomed. He had been framed to kill Lee Harvey Oswald.

Ruby contended up to his death that 'they' had injected him with the cancer. It was not only in his lungs, but in his liver and brain.

This was a real possibility at that time, because every lab in the country had plenty of HeLa cells stored. From 1951 on, every lab had easy access to the HeLa cells that had been found in Henrietta Lack, the cancer cells that could grow at such a rapid rate no matter where they were.

This is not said as definite, but it would be very easy for someone to get their hands on the HeLa cells and inject them into someone spreading a cancer so deadly that could spread like a raging wild fire and get through someone's system so quickly.

The Warren Commission

It doesn't make logical sense to anyone that there were five investigations into Jack F. Kennedy's assassination and into his autopsy evidence and each group still get it wrong. Except, if they were told how they would interpret it to begin with.

Even a person with no medical or forensic science knowledge or background would know that the evidence they put in front of the public was bogus.

There was the:

1. The Warren Commission
2. The Warren's Autopsy Examination

3. The Justice Department's Investigation of the Medical & Autopsy Evidence
4. The Clark Panel
5. The Rockefeller Commission
6. The House Select Committee on Assassinations

The Warren Commission was a joke. It was made up of men who specifically wanted to cover up the conspiracy. President Johnson made sure of it. Those serving on the committee were:

- Earl Warren, Chief Justice of U.S.
- Richard Russell, U.S. Senator
- John Sherman Cooper, U.S. Senator
- Hale Boggs, U.S. Representative
- Gerald Ford, U.S. Representative
- Allen Dulles, former Director of CIA

- John McCloy, former president of World Bank
- 14 assistant counsel members
- 10 staff members

Chief Justice Earl Warren did not want to be any part of this committee. He turned down the offer to be chair multiple times.

Earl Warren was a close friend of the Kennedy's and he suppressed some of the key evidence from the committee. He did not let them see some of the autopsy photos. He tried to stop them from talking to Jackie Kennedy.

He did not want the family put through any more heartache than they had already been through. Don't think the family was stupid, they knew right away who was orchestrating this who assassination.

The commission had secret meetings with Fidel Castro to clear him of any wrong doing. Castro was very upset when he heard of the assassination as he knew he would immediately be the first suspect.

Castro felt that he and Kennedy were beginning to work together and was upset that this even had happened.

The CIA (Central Intelligence Agency) and the FBI (Federal Bureau of Investigation) misled the Warren Commission intentionally about their knowledge of Oswald. It was said that J. Edgar Hoover 'lied his eyes out' to the Commission.

Gerald Ford was 'the leak' from the Warren Commission to the FBI and to J. Edgar Hoover.

The autopsy examination is clear and has some gruesome photos available today that I am not sure were available to the public until recently. In 1963 no one would ever have allowed those photos to be seen by the public. But, with what has become 'acceptable' to view on televisions today and the video games that are played, these pictures would be considered nothing.

The pictures are clear and depict what happened and there is no way a single bullet as the Warren Commission declares to this day, did all this horrific damage.

The Clark Panel was a sub-committee of the Warren Commission. They were requested to review the autopsy findings by The Honorable Ramsay Clark.

For two days, two Professors of Pathology, one Professor of Forensic Pathology and one Professor of Radiology reviewed everything in regards to medical evidence of the assassination.

Their conclusion being that President John Kennedy was hit by not one, but two bullets. Both bullets fired from behind him and above him. One of the bullets went through his neck and the other through his skull at the back imploding inside and causing his skull to explode on the right.

If you can remember, live film the day of the accident when you see Jackie trying to crawl out of the back seat and on to the back of the car, she was trying to retrieve a piece of his skull. She told the secret service agent he would need that.

There is one egregious mistake that runs a bright red thread through all the investigations. John F. Kennedy's body left Dallas without an autopsy or photo's being taken and performed there. His body never should have been allowed to leave without x-rays, photos, and a post-mortem.

This was a gross miscarriage of justice. It should not have mattered if he was the president of the United States. This left so many openings for so much cover up that it leaves a bad taste in anyone's mouth.

After Watergate, all the abuses by the CIA, FBI and other agencies of "intelligence" were finally coming to light. President Ford had Vice-President Nelson Rockefeller (that is the fox watching the hen house) to head up a committee on CIA activities.

The Executive Director was no other than former Warren Commission staffer, David Belin. The Rockefeller Commission also took another look, limited as it was at the John F. Kennedy assassination.

The Commission was there to deal with allegations about Frank Sturgis and Howard

Hunt and the roles that they played in the assassination.

Then, out of the blue, the Rockefeller Commission was replaced by the congressional Church Committee before the Rockefeller Commission even got anything done.

The Rockefeller Commission was worthless. Oh my, did I say worthless. More government dollars wasted I am afraid; to prove nothing, again.

The Church Committee was headed by Senator Frank Church. They looked at the finding of the reports of the Warren Commission and how well the FBI and CIA had worked with the commission. The

Church Committees findings were: that it indicated to them that all the investigation that had been done into the assassination was deficient.

No matter what findings came forth, it did not matter; the Warren Commission held fast that there was only one bullet that did all the damage to Kennedy and Connally. They had to make it one bullet so they could frame Oswald was guilty even though he was a poor shot.

The Warren Commission maintains that one bullet went through John F. Kennedy's neck and on through Governor Connally's chest and his wrist and came to rest in his thigh. That means, the bullet went through 15 layers of cloth, 15 inches of tissue, 7 layers of skin, thru a necktie knot, shattered a radius bone, and removed 4 inches of rib. Their theory also was, that the bullet fell out of Connally's leg onto the gurney at the hospital.

As doctors in the operating room confirmed, the "bullet" remained in Governor Connally's leg.

It is said that the single bullet theory was not fabricated until six months after the fact. For the first few months everyone thought Oswald had shot three shots and that all of them were hits.

In a phone conversation that was taped without knowledge of Lyndon Johnson and J. Edgar Hoover; Hoover tells Johnson that there were three shots fired indeed. That John F. Kennedy was shot with the first and third and Connally shot with the second.

Connally was shot in his back, his leg and his wrist. John F. Kennedy was shot twice in the head, front and back and then once in his back. And then the guy under the overpass that got hit by concrete from a stray bullet hitting the curb. Oops, that was not supposed to happen. That makes it a total of seven shots. There were several guys shooting that day and it is doubtful that Oswald was among them.

They gave the name to the bullet 'CE399' for identifications sake – the Magic Bullet that came through everything and was virtually unscathed, the bullet that did all the damage and killed the President.

I am about to tell you a little piece of an autobiography of Chauncey Holt who died in 1997.

He said a guy by the name of John Masen wanted us to reload several hundred bullets for him. He had unusual orders of how he wanted them reloaded. The bullets were 163 grain and looked like they had never been fired. John said when he looked closer he realized that they had been shot, but there was barely any sign whatsoever that would lead you to believe this was the case.

The master re-loader felt that the bullets had probably been "cold shot"; which means being fired and only using a strong primer, and using no powder.

The 6.5 bullets were then reloaded in their .263 Wetherby cases.

Holt went on to say that they took care and cleaned out the grooves and lands inside a Wetherby rifle that was chambered for a .263. By making these changes, it would look like the bullets had been shot from a Carcano rifle. The very kind of rifle Oswald owned.

The House Select Committee on Assassinations in 1976 decided to take another look at the John F. Kennedy assassination. The committee started out with troubles. There was so much squabbling and fighting amongst the members. Some resigned and had to be replaced and then it had to start all over again. It was a mixed-up mess like the Tower of Babylon.

But one thing this committee did agree on; the Warren Commission did a poor job. That on the day of the assassination whoever was responsible for security of the president did a terrible job. The CIA and FBI were not doing their job as it should have been done on that day and at the time. They did however feel that there was more than likely a conspiracy.

When President Harry S. Truman was in office he formed the CIA. He wanted this agency so that he could have first-hand knowledge of what was going on around the world. They were not to take any kind of covert action, kill anyone or make any decisions. Just keep the president informed of everything going on in all corners of the world and bring this information back to the President and the President only.

After leaving office, Harry Truman regretted forming this agency. He said they had gotten out of control and felt they could decide who to kill and when they should kill. That was not what they were designed to do.

In the beginning, they had worked so well, but now, they were out of control killers, deciding for themselves who should live or die.

One must wonder what Harry Truman would think of the CIA today.

Zapruder Film

Abraham Zapruder was just a good old boy out making a living as a co-owner of a Dallas clothing manufacturer and he was an amateur filmmaker. On this day, November 22, 1963, he didn't bring his best movie camera to work. His secretary urged him to go home and get it. Zapruder dashed to his house and got his Bell & Howell movie camera.

Zapruder captured the whole assassination with his camera. Something no one else had done. Before investigators could get their hands on it, Life Magazine had already bought the rights. The film could prove the shots fired the sequence and the timing.

The Warren Commission, even knowing their statements were not true, stated that the Zapruder film got the entire picture as it rounded the corner and proceeded down Elm Street. This was NOT the case; this was NOT true because, Zapruder, afraid he was going to run out of film, had stopped filming for a few seconds until the president got closer.

Zapruder's film does not help the Warren Commission's theory if you think about it. The film mesmerizes you for sure and may seem deceiving to some, but when it is all said and done, it does not lie.

In the film, about two seconds after the first shot is heard, you can see John F. Kennedy reaching for his neck. He reaches for his neck because the bullet has exited his windpipe and he is having trouble breathing. Jackie is seen supporting his left arm. She is not sure yet what is going on as she thinks what she has heard is a car back firing. You can also see now, Connally's head is turned almost 90 degrees. He has been shot also, through his torso.

No one along the parade route has realized what has happened at this point. The only ones who have realized something is happening is the police on the motorcycles, Jackie, Governor Connally, and the Secret Service on the car behind the President's car.

Agent Hill, seeing John F. Kennedy is in distress, leaps from the cars' running board and tries to cover the president's body with his own.

It is nothing but pure shame that the American people, some of course who never got to know, had to wait the course of 50 years to learn the real truths and find some real answers to questions about John F. Kennedy.

Possible Conspirators

There have been about 2,000 books written on the assassination of President Kennedy. Most of course in regards to the conspiracy that surrounds the assassination. You will find almost no one in America that believes it was a lone shooter. No more than you will find an American who believes that Princess Diana's death was an accident. As soon as American's heard of the shooting, so many felt that it was a conspiracy. No one feels Oswald acted alone and many feel he was not even involved in the shooting.

CIA station chief, E. Howard Hunt had been involved with the failed Bay of Pigs Invasion. He later worked with President

Nixon in the White House. He was detained and questioned after the assassination.

Right before Hunt's death in 2007, he authored a book in which he implicated Lyndon Johnson as the orchestrator of the killing with help from the CIA agents who were mad at Kennedy. The CIA agents were Cord Meyer, Bill Harvey, David Sanchez Morales, David Atlee Phillips, Frank Sturgis, and an unnamed "French gunman" who was the one who supposedly shot from the grassy knoll.

There was Frank Sturgis who had also been involved with the Bay of Pigs and in Watergate. He became romantically involved with Marita Lorenz in 1959 and she turned on him, identifying him as the gunman in the assassination. E. Howard Hunt on his deathbed confession also implicated Sturgis.

Chauncey Holt was said to have been a double agent, acting for the Mafia and for the CIA. He claimed that his assignment while he was in Dallas was to give out fake Secret Service credentials.

David Sanchez Morales, from Cuba supposedly told some of his friends that he was in Dallas when they killed the son of a bitch. He hated the Kennedys. He felt they betrayed his country due to the Bay of Pigs Invasion.

George de Mohrenschildt was the petroleum geologist that was friends with all the oil folks in Texas and a so-called friend of Oswald. He was alleged to be Oswald's CIA handler. In 1976 a representative of the House Select Committee on Assassinations came by, spoke to his daughter, and left his card and said he would be back later that day to talk to George and ask him some questions.

Shortly after seeing the card, he shot himself in the head. His wife told them her husband had been suffering from depression and was afraid of persecution and had tried to kill himself on four different times in that year alone.

There were many Mafia bosses as well as Cuban exiles who disliked John F. Kennedy. They blamed him for everything; starting with the Bay of Pigs. They sure didn't like his brother Robert Kennedy, with his legal onslaught of organized crime.

And after John F. Kennedy died, Bobby got in the way and had to be rubbed out; again, by the same people. Why don't they learn?

This made them especially mad since many of the Mafia families had worked with Joe Kennedy, John F. Kennedy's father, to get him elected as President.

Bonnano, the son of a New York Mafia boss, stated he realized involvement of Mafia when he saw Ruby kill Oswald on TV. He felt that Ruby was part of the Chicago Mafia group Sam Giancana.

In 2006 there was information released by the FBI that Marcello had confessed to organizing the assassination of John F. Kennedy.

Here we are over fifty years later; now everyone wants credit for the killing or for masterminding the assassination. They are coming out of the graves pointing fingers.

There is Dallas Policeman J.D. Tippit who has been named as part of the conspiracy theories. Supposedly he was a renegade CIA agent that was sent to shut up Oswald. He was the "badge man" assassin who was supposedly on the grassy knoll. Some think that Oswald was to be killed by Tippit, but the tables turned and Oswald killed Tippit first. Then there are others that feel Tippit was killed by other conspirators.

Jump to 1995, there was evidence published that both FBI and CIA had tampered with files on Oswald; before and after the death of the President. It was also noted that information was withheld that could have alerted Dallas authorities about the possible threat that Oswald posed towards the president.

It was revealed that CIA chief at the time, James Angleton served as the key figure in the entire assassination plot. He was the only one who had access, authority, and an ungodly ingenious mind to be able to manage a plot this sophisticated. He had to admit though, that the 'cover operation' had to fall under Allen Dulles, 'former CIA director' let go by who else? John F. Kennedy after the Bay of Pigs fiasco.

There is one conspiracy theory that bleeds into all or some of the other theories and that is one called the "shadow government conspiracy". It is one where a 'secret' government that includes right-wing politicians and wealthy industrialists were the ones who ordered the assassination. By doing so, it let them reverse some of the policies and escalate the Vietnam involvement military wise.

While this theory is highly possible, and it involves all those it suggests, plus all the others that have been put into play in this disaster of a plot. Of course, they think that deplorable such as we would not be able to figure any of this out.

Some argue that John F. Kennedy had planned on ending the United States involvement in the Vietnam War; so, he was targeted by people who had special monetary interest in staying in the war. This included the Pentagon and the defense contractors.

There are those who say that lack of Secret Service protection while touring through Dallas was Kennedy's own fault, because that is how he had wanted it. Again, another falsehood exposed.

Vince Palmara interviewed the agents that were assigned to President Kennedy. The driver told him that removing the bubble from the top of the limo, reducing the number of Dallas motorcycle cops near the limo, not having agents positioned beside the limo's rear bumper – none of those orders were made by Kennedy.

If the driver knew that Kennedy had not given the order for all three of these key protection acts, then he had to know who did.

Why was this never documented anywhere for the world to know? Who in fact gave the order for these changes and for the almost near stop in front of the Library?

It is suggested that individual Cuban exiles may have acted alone and be involved with the assassination, but not as a group. This does not feel right even on a bad day. However, there could be individual Cuban's helping with the plot and being paid to assist.

In 2006 information was released that the FBI had held information where Carlos Marcello told his cellmate in Texas, who unbeknownst to Carlos, was an FBI informant and was wearing a bug; stated that he organized John F. Kennedy's assassination. He went on to say that the FBI had the information and covered it up.

An investigative reporter by the name of Jack Anderson stated that organized crime worked with Castro to collaborate the Kennedy assassination.

Critics that disliked the Warren Commission feel strongly that Lyndon Johnson was the person who was behind plotting and planning this devious, horrible act of killing the president. He hated the Kennedy's and was afraid he would not be on the Democratic ticket for the 1964 election.

It was fact that John F. Kennedy wanted to drop Lyndon and was considering seriously taking Johnson off the ticket and replacing him with North Carolina Governor, Terry Sanford.

In the television documentary series, The Men Who Killed Kennedy, when it named the men, oh my goodness, the rage turned to wrath. Anger came from Lyndon Johnson's family, from his former aides, former Presidents Gerald Ford and Jimmy Carter.

Because of the outrage, the History Channel formed a committee of historians, reviewed everything, and decided that the accusations in the documentary had no merit. The History Channel then apologized and said they would not air the series again.

No one will ever know if in fact that there was no merit, or if some felt that they too may be targets for people in high places.

Madeleine Brown, Lyndon Johnson's mistress, said he was in on the conspiracy to kill Kennedy. Madeleine said at a party the night before the assassination that LBJ told her that the Kennedy's would never embarrass him again and that was a fact.

When 1967 rolled around, Lyndon Johnson's polls on popularity had bottomed out. In March 1968, he announced he would not seek re-election for President.

His wife, Lady Bird stated he went into a deep depression about the Vietnam War. How can we know that? How do we not know he was not feeling guilty for all the parts he had played in an assassination of a man who was going to try and end a war? Trying to perform his duties as President of the United States.

A man who was popular with the people and a man who was going to try and make America great again.

Johnson died in 1973, from another heart attack. Few in the United States mourned his passing. He and those he associated with had little value for life.

In 2006, others were coming forward to back up statements.

Some Conspiracy theorists still hang on the thought that Fidel Castro ordered that Kennedy be killed to retaliate for all the attempts to kill him. At one point in the Warren Commissions investigation, a lawyer by the name of William Coleman met with Castro face to face on a fishing boat for a three-hour talk off the island of Cuba. Castro said over and over that he nothing to do with it. There were never any notes taken of this secret rendezvous; and until now, only Earl Warren and another investigator were ever made aware of it at the time.

Some people have conspiracy theories that the Soviet Union, being led by Nikita Khrushchev was responsible for the assassination. They feel he would have been motivated because during the Cuban Missile Crisis, he is the one who backed down.

The Federal Reserve did not even escape its part in being involved in the conspiracy. Per the author of Crossfire, when Kennedy issued his Executive Order 11110 to transfer power from the Federal Reserve over to

United States Treasury and replacing the
Federal Reserve Notes with silver
certificates. If you think about this theory, at
best it is ludicrous.

1963 Meets 2016

Questions arise about a man by the name of Rafael Cruz, Sr. He happens to be the father of Rafael Cruz, Jr., (Ted Cruz), maybe you have heard of him during the Presidential primaries of last year, 2016.

Based on the Sr.'s presence and being an anti-Castro activist, and being in Dallas and in New Orleans before the assassination of John F. Kennedy, there is felt a strong link that Cruz had ties to the CIA.

Rafael Cruz, Sr. weaves a messy web of his life's story. He says he left Cuba in 1957 for the United States. He makes claims that he fought along with Castro against the fascist government but then he soured on the revolution. But in truth, he left Cuba two years before the revolution ever took place.

Then he arrives in Texas, where he gets enrolled at the University of Texas. While he says, he left Cuba with only $100 in his pocket, how could he afford to do all the things he did with just $100 in his pocket?

How did he enroll in college with only $100 for instance? He eventually got permanent residency and a degree in math. He married a Julia Garza and they moved to New Orleans after their second daughter was born on November 18, 1962.

Cruz for some reason claimed two addresses while living in New Orleans. It just so happens he was in New Orleans at the same time Oswald was there and living in the exact same neighborhood as Oswald. He worked for an oil company out of New Orleans. His details about his time in New Orleans are very vague.

Cruz and Julia divorced somewhere around 1962 or 1963. This also seems to be clouded in mystery. He had to register for the draft and when he did, he ran to Canada as fast as he could with his second wife, Eleanor Darragh. He started working in Canada for the oil business there, for Zapata Oil, which was the fake name for the CIA front company that was run by no other than George Herbert Walker Bush. Imagine that! George Herbert got around everywhere before he was confined to his wheelchair. If he really is confined to a wheelchair, it is best to not believe anything you hear and only half of what you see.

After the heat let up, and things had cooled down some, he returned to the U.S. illegally with his son "Ted" Cruz.

Oddly enough 'Ted" had connections to get into Harvard and Princeton and went to work right out of college for the Bush Family business. That is where Ted met his wife Heidi, who also worked for the Bush's.

"Oh! What a tangled web we weave, when first we practice to deceive" Sir Walter Scott

She was from Delaware and had graduated from a college in Houston.

Ted Cruz, while running for President in 2016, alleges that his mom and dad worked for the same oil company in New Orleans but there is no record of his mother ever having lived in New Orleans during that time. Ted Cruz was born in Canada and did not become a U.S. Citizen until 2013.

So, let's muddy the waters a little bit more. Neil Mallon Pierce Bush, who is the fourth of six children of George Herbert Walker Bush, and black sheep of the Bush family; happens to be the campaign manager for Ted Cruz during his election campaign. Doesn't that seem odd that he would be managing a campaign for someone who was running for president against his brother Jeb Bush? Does anyone else think this does not seem, quite right?

Now, not really for sure who would want Neil Bush managing campaign funds when in 2004, he was in some big trouble and had to pay $49.5 million on a negligence suit in regards to a $1 billion, yes, I said $1 billion collapse in a savings and loan that he was director of in Colorado.

The Bush-Cruz connection is clear. Cruz was the brains when George W. ran for President.

Getting himself lined up as top policy advisor, Ted positioned himself then for Solicitor General in the Bush Family World, but settled for a spot with the Federal Trade Commission.

Ted and Heidi like to think they are really "Bush" family. They have even commented that "Condi" Rice gave us that phony war in Iraq. They have also said that they were the first of the Bush kids to get married.

Heidi then went to work as the Bush U.S. Trade Representative as a top deputy. Then on to work for U.S. Trade Rep. Robert Zoellick, who hired Heidi's membership in the Council on Foreign Relations and a job at Goldman Sachs. The bailed-out bank of Goldman Sachs loaned Cruz $1 million secretly to finance his Senate race. Cruz would also borrow an undisclosed $1 million loan from Citicorp.

Cruz is held, propped up by the puppet masters, the Bushes and others of their kind who are looking toward a one world power;

those who call themselves globalist or illuminati.

Very few remember the airline bombing in Cuba in 1976. It was while Bush was Director of the CIA. Two guys, by the names of Bosch and Posada were convicted in Caracas. Posada escaped from prison in 1985. Bosch gets out of prison in 1987 after, a diplomatic negotiation from non-other but Jeb Bush. When Jeb's dad gets elected as president, suddenly, Bosch gets a presidential pardon.

Are you seeing the pattern here? The Bushes who seem to be the wholesome American family that everyone admires are those who protect terrorists and assassins, and anyone and everyone who helped them kill President Kennedy.

Nixon was tied in by the CEO of Pepsi, Don Kendall. And, it is certain that Nixon and Bush were tight.

We know by proof of declassified memo's that George W Bush was in Dallas the night before the assassination. We know from Lyndon Johnson's mistress, Madeline Brown that Nixon and Hoover were in Dallas that night as well.

Even though George Herbert Walker Bush gets amnesia about the night before the assassination, it is well documented that he too was there in Dallas. As a matter of fact, he was at the Dallas Sheraton Hotel when things went down and happened to make a 'confidential' phone call to the FBI after the fact. There is a lovely paper trail to prove that fact.

Before Jackie Kennedy Onassis's death in 1994, she had begged her son, John-John as she called him to please never fly. The Kennedy's carried such a curse on their family and she felt it followed them. She did not want him to own a magazine and least of all she did not want him to name it 'George'.

This did not stop John Jr. He knew who was responsible for his father's death. He was a very intelligent young man.

He named the magazine "George" after George Herbert Walker Bush. He was pushing it right in Bush's face. He was saying "I know where you live and I know what you did to my father."

In his magazine, it is said that articles would be published that would indirectly point fingers to George Herbert Walker Bush.

This leads conspiracy theorists to believe wholeheartedly that John F. Kennedy Jr. no doubt was killed that day when flying his plane. That it was not due to his number of flying hours, not due to his inexperience, but due to someone tampering with the gauges on his plane or something even more sinister that made it plunge into the depths of the ocean.

Everyone knew if John F. Kennedy Jr. ran for president that he was a shoe-in. The globalists did not want that happening and they knew that he knew too much and he could expose all of them. John F. Kennedy Jr. had to go away, and so they made sure he did, to the bottom of the ocean.

At least it was after his mother's death so she did not have to know about his flying of which she feared so much for him.

Body Tampering, Deaths of Witnesses

Funny isn't it, how moving a body can alter it so much. Well, it seemed to alter President Kennedy's body anyway.

In 1979, sixteen years after the assassination, Robert Groden, a researcher said that there were four autopsy photos that showed the back of Kennedy's head and no doubt they were forged. He felt that a picture of another cadaver's head had been placed over Kennedy's picture depicting that there was a huge exit hole in the back of the head. The head of the HSCA, told him that was absurd and that was the end of it.

Some of the researchers claim that the FBI photos show a distinct bullet hole above the rearview mirror in the windshield of the presidential limo, and a crack in the windshield as well. The FBI also brushed this off saying that it was there before Dallas.

Strangely, in 1993, a man by the name of George Whitaker who was a manager at one of the Ford Company's Plants in Detroit came forward with this bit of information. That, when he went to work November 25, 1963, he noticed the president's limo was there.

It took him by surprise, the president's limo in Detroit, all the way from Dallas? The windshield had been taken out and it had a bullet hole through-and-through from the front side. He was instructed to make a new windshield and install it and destroy the old one, to get rid of it.

There were several medical staff who worked at the Parkland Hospital that reported that a huge part of the back of President Kennedy's head was blown out, this suggesting he had been shot from the front.

There is conflicting testimony in regards to the autopsy that was performed on the president's body. When they examined the brain, which was present physically, and if the photos that had been submitted as evidence were the actual photos taken during the autopsy.

Douglas Horne, Assassination Record Review Board Chief Analyst for Military Records states that he is certain to within 90-95% that the pictures in the archives are not those of JFK's brain. He is supported by Dr. Gary Aguilar who says there was no way it was Kennedy's brain.

A lab technologist by the name of Paul O'Connor stated that the brain had already been removed before it got to Bethesda, and there only little pieces of brain left inside the skull.

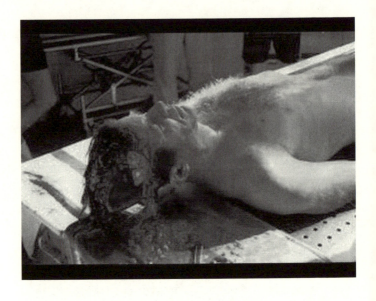

In Dealy Plaza, the day after the
assassination, someone found a bone
fragment and it was supposed to be a part of
John F. Kennedy's parietal bone. Others say
it is really a piece of occipital bone that had
been ejected from the exit wound at the back
side of John F. Kennedy's head.

Those who know this say this is cover-up. It
proves that the x-rays of the skull during the

autopsy, that do not show any significant bone loss in that area, do not belong to John F. Kennedy.

There are unidentified witnesses that have never been located. One they call "umbrella man" was a very close bystander that day when the president was first shot. He was holding an open umbrella on a sunny day and it had not been raining.

At that time, the umbrella could have been used to signal someone or during that year, the CIA had a dart that could be shot from an umbrella that paralyzed, disabling someone, like John F. Kennedy, leaving Kennedy as a sitting duck, so to speak and an easy target.

Then there was the 'dark skinned man' that no one has been able to identify. He was sitting next to 'umbrella man'. This made some speculate about Cuban involvement even more.

'Black dog man' who was at the corner of the retaining wall. This person has never come forward to identify themselves.

November 20, 1963, Jack Ruby's employee Rose Cheramie had been found disoriented and bruised, lying alongside a road in Louisiana. The state trooper that found her, in his report stated that while he was driving her to the hospital, she said she had been left there by two guys who were either Italian or Latin. They had told her that they were going to Dallas to kill the President. The trooper stated she seemed to know what she was talking about and he believed her. The hospital employees that saw her that evening said they too believed her story was credible.

Much of her story about a drug deal going down did check out, due to the fact she was a heroin addict and undergoing withdrawal, her telling everyone of the assassination was not given serious thought. After the assassination, when Dallas Police officials and the FBI were notified, they were not interested.

Odd however, Cheramie was found dead by the side of a highway near Big Sandy, Texas, September 4, 1965, almost two years after the assassination; she had been mowed down by a car.

Joseph Milteer, the director of Dixie Klan of the state of Georgia told Miami police that the killing of Kennedy was in the works. They ignored this as well. However, he died when his hot water heater exploded in his house.

Nationally syndicated columnist, Dorothy Kilgallen had told some of her friends she was following Jack Ruby's trial. She gained a private meeting with Ruby, and after being hounded for months by the FBI, Dorothy was found dead in her Manhattan home having died mysteriously.

When the body count of witness's that came up missing is tallied, it adds up to somewhere around fifty. That is at least fifty people who had to be shut up.

Why was so much evidence suppressed? Because they already had their answers and they simply did not want to listen to what anyone else had to tell.

In 1967, a Josiah Thompson declared that the Warren Commission just ignored seven witness's testimony who had seen gun smoke near the grassy knoll that day and eight witnesses who had smelled gunpowder.

In 1989, it was realized the Commission had not even interviewed witnesses who had been standing on the overpass who had statements that pointed to the fact there was a shooter on the grassy knoll.

Everyone with a movie camera or camera had their cameras seized that day. That alone speaks conspiracy! The Zapruder film slipped through their fingers though. Ha-Ha!

There are still documents in regards to the assassination that are not due to be released until 2029. That should be a good time to release them, by that time, anyone still interested in the real conspiracy should be dead by then.

Conclusion

There are many who feel that the assassination of John F. Kennedy was long ago and we just need to forget about it. The interest therein should just be left alone. It is time to move on.

I do not agree. Since it has changed our political landscape forever, it is very relevant today and for the future of our children. If we are truthful to ourselves, we will admit that our political problems tie back to that fateful day of November 22, 1963. That the globalist, the Illuminati whatever they call themselves, the ones wanting the "One World" power structure; a one world leader and are still working toward that end. Is that something we want for future generations?

So, I ask you this question. If you had to decide right now, after reading this book, who do you think gave orders to shoot the smoking guns?

The world will never know who the persons were that gave the "official" order to kill John F. Kennedy for those persons are either already dead, close to death, silent in fear of death, or they choose to remain silent until death.

1999 ~ Robert G. Vernon

Jackie Kennedy Onassis

A Jackie Kennedy Biography

Katy Holborn

Introduction

When we think of how we would like to be remembered, many things will come to mind. Perhaps for our family, maybe for things we have achieved, for our kindness, or for our understanding, and empathy.

Though, for Jackie Kennedy, recognition comes mostly from one day in November 1963, her involvement in a defining event which fixes her in the public eye.

Despite the fact that she would go on to achieve much more in her life and prior to that day had built up a promising career. That one afternoon in Texas, when her husband President John F Kennedy was assassinated, is the abiding image of a life well lived.

This book will look at that dreadful day, but will also show that Jackie Bouvier, later Kennedy then Onassis, should be remembered for more than just one single, terrible event.

We will consider her childhood, growing up in a privileged but troubled environment. The early career she abandoned to become one of the most famous and influential women on earth.

We will look at the consequences of these three wicked bullets, not just for a nation, but also for a grieving human with two small children.

The circumstances around the decision to marry one of the world's richest man in her later years, maybe her happiest, before her own untimely death.

This book will show the reader that there was much more to Jackie Kennedy than a bloodied pink suit and an open topped drive through Dallas, Texas.

Chapter One – A Beautiful Baby

Jacqueline Lee Bouvier was born into a well-off family in Southampton, New York, on July 28th 1929.

John Bouvier, her father, was a wealthy stock broker who worked on Wall Street. His own family had immigrated to the US from France in the early 1800s.

Her mother was a New York Socialite. Janet Bouvier came from Irish descent, and was the daughter of a Manhattan lawyer and real estate developer.

Her mother was also a talented horse rider, something in which Jackie would soon herself develop a healthy and successful interest.

But the marriage was not a happy one. Beneath the façade of wealth, partying and membership of the highest echelons of society, trouble lurked like a blocked pipe in a luxury hotel, occasionally to pour its odor into unwanted places.

John Bouvier was a notorious womanizer and heavy drinker. He was also a gambler, and one whose own forays into the stock market brought differing results.

Following the birth of their two daughters (Jackie's younger sister, Caroline, was born in 1933) the inevitable happened, and they separated.

This was 1936, and Caroline was just three years old. However, John and Janet tried again the following year, and got back together for a while. But matters did not work out, and the Bouviers were eventually divorced in 1940.

John Bouvier had a rather spending full name. John Vernou Bouvier III. But he was known as 'Black Jack', due to his rugged good looks, permanent tan and hard living lifestyle.

He was born in East Hampton, New York in May 1891 to a successful attorney, but trace back further and his French heritage is revealed.

Michel Bouvier immigrated to Philadelphia following Napoleon's defeat in the battle of Waterloo.

There, he opened a successful cabin making store, and made fine furniture for the local landowners.

In order to do this, he decided to buy large tracts of forest, which he also used to supply his second business, one that distributed firewood.

Bizarrely, his wealth would come more from this venture than his artistic side. And that was down more to luck than judgement. It turned out that the forest land he had purchased was based above vast pits of coal, and that ground was worth a fortune.

This was the family money that John Bouvier would later use, and mostly lose, to help fund his extravagant lifestyle, and that of his wife.

For a while, his Wall Street successes gave that money a boost, but as John's alcoholism grew, so expenditure began to outstrip income, and the fortune started to disappear.

John's brother died of alcoholism and it seems as though it was a problem from which John also suffered.

At his daughter's wedding to Kennedy, reports claim that he was too inebriated to escort her down the aisle, and her step father, Hugh Dudley Auchincloss Jr had to step in.

However, other stories also exist which say that it was his ex-wife, Janet, who persuaded Jackie to be accompanied by her step-father. In these accounts, it was never the plan for John to perform the task.

More likely, though, it was simply that he was drunk. We know that, despite his problems, he remained close to both of his daughters.

Bouvier eventually became remote from his former, and spent more and more time

drinking alone in his New York apartment.
Given the grand places in which he had been
brought up, and lived in with his family, this
was a wretched place.

It had just one bedroom, and a box room into
which the daughters squeezed when they
stayed over. Days started and ended with a
drink, and indeed alcohol occupied most of
the remainder of his day.

The former wild living man became a virtual
recluse. He contracted liver cancer and died
in hospital on July 27th, 1957.

Jackie was the one who organized his
funeral.

To return to Jackie's mother, Janet, she remained married to her second husband until his death in 1976. She married for a third time three years later.

This time, it was to a childhood friend, Bingham Willing Morris, and Jackie served as a witness at this wedding. Ironically. Bingham's late wife had been a bridesmaid at Janet's marriage to John Bouvier.

Janet contracted Alzheimer's disease, and died in 1989.

So, we can see that Jackie was born into a life where her parents fought, drank and socialized. For all of this, Jackie's childhood was good.

She started her education at Miss Chapin's School in New York, where her teachers described her as pretty, extremely clever and very artistic.

Indeed, Jackie had learned to read well before starting school, and consumed books quickly. She loved Kipling's The Jungle Book, Robin Hood and Little Lord Fauntleroy.

Right from these early days, Janet Bouvier predicted that her daughter would end up as some kind of writer.

Miss Chapin's school, an exclusive institution attended by the children of the rich, had a reputation for being slightly different.

It encouraged work with the environment; although based in the heart of a great city. The school compensated for its lack of green surroundings with greenhouses, the upkeep of which formed part of the curriculum for the younger children.

Miss Chapin herself was a bit of a maverick. She founded the school at the turn of the 20th Century, and was an early supporter and promoter of the rights of women.

She was a suffragette, and although she had recently stepped down as the Head teacher before Jackie joined the school, her influence still pervaded the corridors.

It seems like an ideal school for a free-thinking girl such as Jackie Bouvier.

Despite this, as pretty and clever as she might be, Jackie was a bit of a tearaway at school, getting herself into trouble.

She was once excluded from her Geography class and sent to see the Headmistress because of her disruptive behavior.

She followed her mother's interest in equestrianism and by the age of eleven was winning tournaments regularly. She even appeared in the New York Times.

'Jacqueline Bouvier, an eleven-year-old equestrienne from East Hampton, Long Island, scored a double victory in the horsemanship competition,' read the report. 'Miss Bouvier achieved a rare distinction.

The occasions are few when a young rider wins both contests in the same show.'

But this was also one of the lowest points in her childhood. Her parents had just divorced, and that was a rarity in the Catholic world in which they lived.

The church disapproved of divorce, and for a while Jackie withdrew into herself. However, she continued to be a busy young girl, taking up ballet alongside her horse riding.

When her mother married for the second time, her family grew, as she gained some step siblings – two brothers and a sister.

She went to board at Miss Porter's School, which was for girls and was based in Connecticut. She left there at age seventeen, and attended Vassar College at home in New York, where she studied literature, history, art and French – evidence that her loves had changed little during her childhood.

She spent a year also studying in Paris, at the world-famous Sorbonne, and her time in the city of art and culture was one of the highlights of her life to that point.

She loved Europe – something that would remain with her for life – but also gained greater insights into herself during her time in France.

She had been educated during a period, and among a class of girls, where a thirst for knowledge was not really celebrated. This had especially been the case at her boarding school.

Education was more about learning to be a good wife, than developing one's own intellect and curiosity.

It was still a man's world, and any girls bright enough to challenge this were shaped into a less threatening state.

This was particularly true among a class of girls who would become the socialites and wealthy wives of the US's most advantaged young men.

So, while her thirst for knowledge had been recognized in her US schooling, that recognition was tempered with a sense that it was not totally the right thing upon which a girl of Jackie's ilk should focus upon.

The situation was different in Paris, and Jackie learned to see her own thirst for learning as something in which to take pride, rather than slightly hide away.

She returned to New York to complete her education. But by now the United States, post war, was starting to recognize that it was a time where the role of women was beginning to change.

A career was becoming an acceptable, even desirable option, even for the super-rich. A life of partying and socializing was no longer the only choice for such women.

And her mother's prediction proved to be right. Jacqueline took her first job, and she became a writer – a journalist for the Washington Times-Herald.

Chapter Two – The Inquiring Photographer

Jackie Bouvier's career as a journalist was not especially long – she became side tracked by something more significant as we shall see – but she certainly got around.

Her role was as a journalist photographer. She would take pictures of events and people, interview them and write up the reports. The Washington Times Herald called her their 'Inquiring Camera Girl', and paid her the princely sum of $42.50 a week for her work.

She would head out onto the streets armed with a topical question, which she would pose to members of the general public. Their responses formed the basis of a daily feature.

Mostly, she supplied what we might call the gossip column in today's media; and her writing was not considered among the most important parts of the paper – she did not even get her own by-line.

She started as a twenty-two-year-old rookie, but her promise was recognized, and she soon found herself involved in some major events.

One of her first bigger jobs came when she was invited to interview and photograph Irish diplomats who were in Washington for St Patrick's Day in 1952.

She had been in post for only around six months at this point. She was dispatched to the Irish Assembly to pose the question, 'What to you is the significance of St Patrick's Day?'

The then ambassador, John Hearne, offered a safe response. 'First and last it is a religious feast, the rededication of our people to the religious faith and moral traditions identified with the Irish race for a thousand years.'

For Bouvier, though, it was a more important assignment than most. She had visited Ireland a couple of years previously, and her Irish ancestry (on her mother's side) had made her feel at home immediately.

The article she wrote still did not get her a by-line, but it did provide her with an even greater interest in her Irish ancestry.

Later, she wrote to her friend and mentor Father Joseph Leonard. She had met the Dublin priest on her earlier visit.

'They were so sweet' she said of the Irish politicians. Hearing their accents had reminded her of her time in Ireland, and had been an emotional experience for her.

In under a year, she had moved considerably up the paper's hierarchy. In January, she was sent to cover the inauguration of the new President, Dwight D Eisenhower, who was about to become the 34th US President.

Then, later in the same year, she was sent overseas for another major world event, the coronation of the current Queen of England and the Commonwealth, Elizabeth II.

That was an even more spectacular occasion, with all the pomp and color that the British do so well.

But while she was there, she received a phone call that would signal the end of her burgeoning career in journalism.

To understand these, we need to move backwards in time.

Back in the fall of 1951, when she had just started out on her new career, she met – socially – a promising young politician.

That initial meeting was not particularly life changing, Jackie was in a stable if not especially invigorating relationship at the time, but within a year the politician and the journalist, each with their stars rising, had fallen in love.

And it was while Jackie was in England, covering the new Queen's enthronement that the phone call came.

A proposal of marriage from that same young politician; a proposal she gladly accepted.

As we can all guess, the politician in question was future president, member of the powerful Kennedy family and notorious womanizer, a man known to all as JFK.

Chapter Three – A Promising Politician

John Fitzgerald Kennedy was born on the 29th of May 1917, while the Great War in Europe moved towards its most muddy and bloody latter stages.

He was the second child of Joseph Kennedy Sr and Rose Kennedy, and would eventually have eight siblings in his Catholic family.

Joseph was an ambitious and able man, who had married into the wealth of the Irish Catholic Upper Class in Boston. Rose was the daughter of the city's popular mayor.

Joseph's big break came when he was working at a bank in the city. A Boston shipyard, which was busily churning out warships for the conflict across the Atlantic, needed a new manager.

He was the perfect man for the job. From there, Joseph began to make money from his own initiatives, investing in the new and rapidly growing movie theatre industry.

He even went as far as Hollywood, both buying and selling various movie companies in those early days of cinema.

From there, he entered Wall Street, making a series of highly successful moves in the stock market. He was one of the very few people to still make money following the 1929 Wall Street Crash.

By the 1930s, when John was still a teenager, the family had become seriously wealthy; Rose's family fortune being more than matched by the money Joseph had made.

He moved into politics, donating considerable funds to the Democratic Party and in the process became a close associate of Franklin D Roosevelt, although he would later fall out with the wartime President.

After the war, he established trust funds of at least ten million dollars for his numerous children, and amassed a personal fortune of up to four hundred million dollars.

The Kennedy dynasty was established.

But back to John's early years, growing up wealthy was one thing, but in Protestant dominated Boston, Catholic families were still considered socially inferior.

He and his elder brother attended a prestigious school, which was the institution of choice for the offspring of the rich white protestant community that sat at the summit of East coast society in those days.

That community had kept the likes of the Kennedys and the Fitzgerald's (Rose's family) out of the exclusive country clubs.

Perhaps that need to prove himself was a part of what drove Joseph on. Whether so or not, it made him drive into his children ambition and deep family unity.

They siblings were expected to compete internally, but the family reputation was all, and when push came to shove they were to close shop and stick together to preserve the Kennedy name.

This was something we would see time and again when tragedy following tragedy hit the family.

They were also to be socially and academically aspirational, and Joseph ensured that they drove their own political ambitions from an early age.

As we know in retrospect, such drive would come to make the Kennedy family immensely powerful in US politics. Beginning from Joseph's rise in the 1930s the family dominated the political landscape for forty years through subsequent generations.

Even today, family members are active in the political arena.

The family moved to New York and John was entered into a highly exclusive school – Choate – a school so conservative that Jews were excluded, and Catholics only borne with extreme reluctance.

There, John was less successful than he would have wished. He regularly got into trouble, and academically was in the shadow of his older brother.

That Kennedy charm, however, was immediately apparent.

'When he flashed his smile, he could charm a bird off a tree,' his Headmaster recalled.

At this time, John often felt that he was forever following in his brother's footsteps, and that applied not only to his education, but also the eyes of his father.

Later, when his brother was killed in action in a war time flying incident, it would be to John that his father directed his primary ambitions.

But that was still to come.

During the latter part of the 1930s, Joseph Kennedy was appointed ambassador to Great Britain.

Young John began his own early forages into politics at this time, using his father's position to organize tours of Europe, where he would stay at the homes of ambassadors, and report back his findings on Europe to his father.

John was in England when war broke, and on his return to the US, where he was studying at Harvard, his experience led him to publish a thesis on appeasement.

With his father's influence, the paper became widely read and gained a popular authority. John F Kennedy's name was starting to emerge in political circles.

That name grew in status when he was on active service during the war. He gained control of a small torpedo boat, was rammed in the Pacific by a Japanese warship and saved most of the crew by leading them to a nearby island where they made contact with some native inhabitants.

It was the perfect story for a young man destined for high places.

Soon, though, the tragedies with which the Kennedys would be associated – and which

would impact directly on Jackie Bouvier –
began.

Joseph Jr became a victim of the war.

His father, who had opposed the US entry
into the conflict, went into meltdown,
distanced himself from Roosevelt, criticizing
him for links with 'Jews and Communists'
and put all his energy into ensuring that
John would get the political career he had
planned for his eldest son.

The next opportunity for this arose near to
John's first home, in Massachusetts. A seat
in the House of Representatives became
available. The area it represented was
overwhelmingly poor, full of Irish and

Italian Catholics, and bound to be a Democrat shoe-in.

Joseph Kennedy pulled every string, called in every favor and promoted his son endlessly to ensure that he would secure the Democrat nomination.

John, by now widely known as JFK, was a man often hit by illness, but despite this he had vigor and charm, and with such support his victory was straight forward.

That illness was soon to be diagnosed. In fact, he had an incurable glandular disorder called Addison's disease. Cortisone injections helped, and he began to fill out and look healthier.

His war time exploits had also damaged his back, leading to incapacitating bouts of pain.

However, the family closed ranks to keep the problems secret. Nothing could be allowed to risk the family reputation or JFK's rise in the political arena, even something as unavoidable as an illness.

People liked their leaders to be full of health and that was the impression, Joseph Kennedy believed, that they had to hold of his son.

Despite the charm, the intellect and the string pulling behind the scenes, JFK had another weakness alongside the physical one he endured.

He was a man who found at least one thing as attractive as political power; John Kennedy was inextricably drawn to the opposite sex, and had become an increasingly active womanizer.

As well as the moral duplicity of such activities, he also occasionally displayed poor judgement.

He became friends with another young politician, an outspoken Republican called Joseph McCarthy, who would (along with Richard Nixon) become one of America's most reviled political leaders of all time.

In 1951, he met an attractive young journalist called Jackie Bouvier and as, in 1952, that relationship began to bloom, so he ran for a place on the US Senate.

Against the mood of the nation at the time, with Republicanism enjoying a wave of popularity, but with his father's considerable and powerful support, he won that race.

The new Senator for Massachusetts was one John Fitzgerald Kennedy.

The young man's illness was in check, his political life was thriving, and finally, he was properly in love.

Chapter Four – The Rise and Fall of 'Camelot'

The relationship that grew between the young Jackie – she was just twenty-three when they married – and the older politician was complex in the extreme.

But it was based on love. Letters she sent to her Irish priest confidant, Father Leonard, illustrated that.

And they offered insight into the intelligence of the beautiful woman. She understood that being married to a politician, a leading one at that, was different to the norm.

'Maybe I'm just dazzled and picture myself in a glittering world of crowned heads and Men of Destiny – and not just a sad little housewife,' she wrote.

But with a clear perception of her life ahead once she committed to the Kennedy clan, she continued: 'That world can be very glamourous from the outside – but if you're in it – and you're lonely – it could be a Hell.'

John F Kennedy never saw marriage as a reason to stop his philandering ways – relationship followed relationship, most notably, of course, with the troubled actress Marilyn Monroe.

But for the wife, through the 1950s and into the early 1960s, she was still expected to be there as a support for her husband.

She was expected to behave in the right way, wear the correct clothing, keep her intelligence to herself and stand by her man, whatever he got up to.

Jackie was engaged to a stock broker, John Husted, when she first met JFK. They had each been invited to a dinner hosted by mutual friends, and the attraction was immediate to the young senator.

He asked her out for a drink, but backed off when he discovered that she was already engaged.

However, that relationship was already dying – she found Husted 'too immature', and her mother felt that he was not the right man for her daughter.

But within a couple of months of ending the engagement, Jackie was heading for that drink.

For JFK, according to Jackie, the thrill behind his womanizing was always the chase. Once he attained his goal, he was ready to move on to somebody else.

However, it seemed not to be the situation on this occasion, John besotted by his younger girlfriend, and the two were soon engaged,

That this took place by phone call, when Jackie was in England covered Queen Elizabeth's coronation, would suggest that it was a genuine love from JFK.

Otherwise, why bother to make the call when his future wife is halfway across the world?

The couple was wed in a lavish ceremony with a thousand guests just three months later.

On September 12th 1953, at St Mary's Church on Rhode Island, they held the ceremony, before moving to her mother's vast Victorian home for the reception.

The controlling influence of the Kennedy family, the patriarchal Joe in particular, was already being felt by Jackie, though. She disliked her wedding dress, into which the Kennedy clan has 'contributed' several design ideas.

John's war time back injury returned with a vengeance soon after their wedding. He felt it needed to be sorted once and for all.

Surgery would be the only answer. But his other condition, the Addison's disease from which he still suffered, led his blood pressure to drop during surgery and he fell into a coma. It appeared that he could die without recovering consciousness.

He was even given the last rites. But he pulled through, and Jackie persuaded him to write a book about US senators to fill the long days during his recovery.

That book, Profiles in Courage (about politicians who had made a difference with their works), would go on to win the Pulitzer Prize.

Perhaps it was the closeness of death, or maybe just a young couple entering the next stage of their life, but they decided it was time to start a family.

However, that too would prove to be difficult. Jackie fell pregnant in 1955, but miscarried. Then, the following year, she gave birth to a stillborn baby, who they called Arabella.

They were still recovering from that tragic event when JFK's political career took another step forwards. He was nominated to stand as Vice President on the Democratic ticket, with Adlai Stevenson running for President.

However, victory went to the Republican Eisenhower- whom, ironically, Jackie had covered at his inauguration after he won his first Presidential election.

But 1957 proved to be a better year personally for the couple. On November 27th, 1957, Jackie gave birth to their first child, a daughter, whom they named Caroline.

Then, in 1960, JFK announced that he would run for President. Once again, the Kennedy machine came out in force.

But, at the same time, Jackie fell pregnant once again. It meant that she could not accompany her husband on the campaign trail as much as she wished.

But when she needed to be at home, she still supported her husband's ambition with administrative help, giving TV interviews and by writing a weekly column in a newspaper called 'Campaign Wife'.

It may have been unintentional, but the overall impact was positive for his campaign. Instead of just being a presence by his side, Jackie became a second string to his campaign.

The attractive, wealthy young mother, working for her husband as best as she could, struck a nerve with the electorate, and contributed significantly to his subsequent victory.

On the 25th of November, 1960, Jackie gave birth to their second child. A boy, John Jr, who was born just sixteen days after his father won the election to become the next President of the United States of America.

By this point, Kennedy was 43 and Jackie 31. In January of the following year Kennedy was inaugurated as the 35th President and Jackie had the responsibility of a new born baby and a toddler. As well as being the new First Lady.

She hired a secretary to assist with her official duties so that she could concentrate on her role as a mother.

She would later describe her Jack (her name for JFK) as like a Macbeth, such was his overriding ambition to lead and wield power.

The charming, smiling young leader the world saw found the pressures of Presidency greater than he would let on. This often to led to debilitating back pain, despite his operation, and he would often find outlets for these pressures through brief affairs.

Jackie coped, though. Perhaps inspired by the need to bring up two young children in the White House, she set about restoring it to its former glory.

Something that she has been thanked for by future Presidential families ever since. She raised funds and created the White House Historical Association.

She worked with Congress to ensure legislation which would secure the preservation of historic buildings, and created the role of White House Curator.

She made sure that the furniture in the house would remain Federal Government property, tying it in with the Smithsonian Institute.

In early 1962, she invited the TV cameras into the White House so that the country at large could see the work she was leading, and the reasons behind it.

The subsequent show won her an Emmy for public service. She also used the White House to promote Art, a subject she loved.

Displays would be held in the building, featuring the work of American artists, and she used her influence to lobby for National Endowments to support the arts, and humanities.

Despite her busy, multi-faceted lifestyle, despite being married to a man who seemed incapable of stopping his forages into extra marital relationships, she became pregnant for the fifth time.

But once again, it would not be a success. Patrick Bouvier Kennedy was born on August 7th 1963, premature, but lived for only two days.

He was buried next to Arabella, his still born sister. The tragedy brought the couple closer together, but with just three months left of life for JFK, that extra warmth was short lived.

On that fateful November day in 1964, they landed in Dallas, Texas, where Jackie was given a bunch of red roses.

On the previous day, she had been presented no fewer than three times with the state's famous yellow roses, but the red ones given in Dallas would stay in her mind.

Soon they would be splattered with the deeper red of her husband's blood. Another image that would last with her throughout her life.

Later, she would wonder if they were a warning of the danger ahead.

The cavalcade progressed through the streets of Dallas, and headed past the bookstore from which Lee Harvey Oswald (if it was he) fired the fateful shots.

The couple had glanced at each other fractionally before the first bullet hit.

Jackie would describe a look of slight confusion on her husband's face as the bullet struck him, and recalled the slow-motion effect of seeing a part of his skull separate from his head.

She leapt for it, climbing onto the back of the open topped car in which they were travelling and grasping it.

Her critics claimed she was trying to save herself, by getting out of the car, but her thoughts were just for her husband.

He had slumped on to her lap when the bullet hit, and as she returned to the car, a security man, Clint Hill, throwing himself onto her as a human shield, she once again hugged her dying husband.

Her gloved hand held firmly onto his head as she attempted to keep his brains from leaking out. Such is the horror of a bullet to the skull.

'I tried to hold the top of his head down, maybe I could keep it in, she said, but I knew he was dead.'

He eyes, as blue as ever, were fixed in a stare, and it was clear he had passed on, but still she clung to hope.

'Jack, Jack, Jack, can you hear me? I love you, Jack, I love you.' Her whispers were intense, and when they reached the hospital seven minutes later she insisted that she stayed with him.

She held a jacket over the wound in his head; it was not right for this corruption to be witnessed by others.

He was taken to Trauma Room One of Parkland Hospital, and two burly doctors tried to bar her from accompanying him into the room.

But she insisted, at first quietly then with increasing volume until they gave way. In her hand, she still clutched the part of his skull she had collected from the car.

She handed it to a doctor. Astonishingly, the President still retained a faint pulse. While doctors desperately worked, with all that they had back in those 50 plus years ago days, she sat outside.

But in the end, knowing the inevitability of his state, she returned to the room to be with him as died.

The chief surgeon, Dr Malcolm Perry, insisted that she leave, but she would not go.

'It's my husband. His blood, his brains is all over me.'

She knelt in prayer, and when she arose all could see her pink outfit soaked in his blood.

At one pm, the doctors could do no more, and covered the President's face with a sheet. Jackie mouthed 'I know' when a doctor confirmed the inevitable. She could not speak.

A foot, white and drained, was exposed, and she bent and kissed it. Then, she kissed his leg, his chest and finally his lips.

His eyes were still open, and Jackie described his mouth as 'so beautiful'. Even the hardened doctors were touched by her gestures.

Three hundred thousand people watched the funeral procession for JFK. The event took place on Sunday November 25th, 1963.

The procession echoed that of another assassinated President, Abraham Lincoln. Although only aged six and three, their two children attend their father's funeral.

After a quick word from his mother, young John Jr saluted his father's coffin as it passed.

The procession, led by the President's coffin in a horse and carriage, continued to St Matthew's Cathedral for the funeral service.

He was then interred in Arlington National Cemetery, where Jackie lit the eternal flame over her Jack's grave.

Chapter Five - Aftermath

Jackie Kennedy was a private person – as much as that is possible to be as a first lady. But a few days after the funeral, she gave an interview to Life Magazine.

With the country still in complete shock, the interview stirred the nation. Under the headline, 'For President Kennedy: An Epilogue' the interviewer Theodore H White, along with some interventions from former journalist Jackie herself, put together a story that the country needed at that time.

Subsequent revelations, allegations, stories and books have cast doubts on the picture Jackie created. The motivations behind the creation of such doubts are difficult to determine. But we will try.

The story created an image of perfection in the Kennedy led Presidency, with John playing the music from Camelot before settling to sleep at night.

His favorite song contained the line: 'Don't let it be forgotten, that once there was a spot, for one brief shining moment that was known as Camelot.'

Jackie went on 'There'll be great Presidents again – and the Johnsons are wonderful, they've been wonderful to me – but there'll never be another Camelot again.'

Later, allegations of everything from the Kennedys being on the verge of divorce, to suggestions of corruption and links with organized crime would be thrown at the regime.

They, though, would never seriously dent the love in which JFK and Jackie are held.

It is bizarre that such criticism should flow to the misty-eyed vision of life in the White House that is portrayed in the interview.

It is just a week since the funeral of JFK and Jackie is still in mourning. She contacts an old journalist friend (White) who had supported John Kennedy on his Presidential campaign trail.

She is hardly going to offer a criticism of a much loved and recently murdered husband.

Following the funeral, Jackie and the children had to vacate the White House for the new incumbents, Lyndon Johnson and his entourage.

Initially they moved into an apartment leant by a friend and close to the one they had previously owned in Georgetown.

But memories were too strong, and after a while they moved once more, this time to New York, where she purchased a 5th Avenue apartment.

For a spell, the shock of the assassination had a terrible, but not unexpected, impact on Jackie. At her lowest, she became suicidal, and could not even face the pain of seeing her husband's face.

She found some solace in alcohol, and discovered that vodka took the pain away. She felt that her children were suffering because of her distress.

People helped as best as they could. She was sent a portrait of her late husband, which she tried to keep. But young John Jr, on seeing it, kissed the painting, saying 'Good night Daddy.'

She told friends that her life was over, and she was only waiting for it to be literally finished through her own death.

She linked her situation to the recently deceased former love of her husband, Marilyn Monroe, who was believed to also have taken her own life.

And she said that she was glad that Marilyn was now at peace, and hoped that she would soon join her.

She was haunted by the assassination. The first shot fired by the assassin had missed the car, so she recalled, and she had thought it was a backfiring vehicle.

She blamed herself for not recognizing the sound for what it was, and protecting her husband in the three and a half seconds between shots.

In the days immediately following the Camelot interview, she had taken the children to Cape Cod to get away from the endless attention.

She decided on who would write an account of her husband's assassination, and settled on an unknown writer, William Manchester. She could not face endless stories relating the same information.

And something that became intensely important to her was that their two dead children, Patrick and Arabella should be reburied with their father.

Normally reserved and under emotional control, she became volatile, berating a friend who praised her for bearing up under the strain of memorial services.

'How did she expect me to behave?' she asked bitterly. She was savage to those who offered the kindly meant words that time would offer some healing.

But through her own personal suffering, through her nightmares and drinking, and her own sense of failing both her husband and now Caroline and John Jr, she worked hard to make things as normal as possible for their young children.

Even though Christmas fell just a little over month after his assassination, Jackie made it as festive as it could be for the children. They followed the traditions they had established when her Jack had been alive.

She had the children's rooms in their new home decorated as they had been in the White House, hoping that familiarity would ease their feelings.

But she particularly disliked the public's designation of her as a heroine. Remember, JFK was a deeply popular president. In Stephen Sondheim's musical 'Assassins', he tells of how people were traumatized by his death, one even committing suicide.

Jackie held herself together in public, and through that the public saw her as a role model, an exemplar of strength and commitment.

'I don't like to hear people say that I am poised and maintaining a good appearance,' she complained to a friend and mentor, Bishop Hannan.

Inside, she continued to blame herself for her husband's death, certain that she should have done more.

Through January, the numbers waiting to see her or the children swelled, and she began to fear for their own safety.

Crowds could mean danger, and already mystery around the motivations regarding her husband's assassination was growing.

Over 10000 people a day were making a pilgrimage to see the President's grave at Arlington, and many were also visiting the grieving family's new house.

Even tour buses included it on their route. At night, the house could be seen into easily from the streets, and no privacy could be gained from the well-meaning, but insensitive hoards who waited on the street.

President Johnson opened the Warren Commission which would investigate all aspects of the assassination.

But for Jackie, she found herself increasingly disinterested. Even if they found out the motivations behind the attack, it would not bring back her husband. In the scheme of things, it would make little difference to life for her and her children.

Meanwhile, she had agreed for a historian, Arthur Schlesinger, to interview her to provide a permanent, inside, record of her Jack's presidency.

It had always been her husband's intention to tell this story when he eventually left the role, and now she felt it was her duty to do it in his place. But for a lady suffering so much, it was a difficult challenge.

Mainly, this challenge is made worse by her own distress at events. But also, Jackie knew that her husband was a man as well as a President. He had his failings, physical and moral, and she had to judge the extent to which these could be told.

She was also putting off the meeting she knew she had to hold with the biographer she had appointed, William Manchester.

And a couple of holidays she took with family and friends, one skiing, one to the Caribbean, were sad and desultory affairs.

Another person who was especially suffering was JFK's brother, Bobby. As Attorney General, he had pursued actions against Cuba and the Mafia, and he feared that the assassination could have been prompted as a form of revenge for these.

Six months after the tragic event, she began to see a priest, father McSorley. This was on the loose pretext that she was a keen tennis player, and he was a good exponent of the game, and could teach her some tricks.

But it was far more a chance for some more counselling. He helped her to realize that her place was with her children, and that they needed her, despite her feelings of failure.

And shortly after these 'lessons', she was able to meet properly with Manchester.

They were difficult times, with Jackie keen to move on and get the event of the assassination out of her head, while he felt the need to get inside the occasion.

She said more than she wished, finding it hard to stop once 'the floodgates open'. That Manchester routinely drip fed her cocktails did not help her control.

The interviews sent her back into despair, and Father McSorley began to worry about her mental health, and the risk of suicide, once more.

In her own words, Jackie had tried to ascend the hill to escape the valley of her despair, but after a few steps had tumbled back down to it. The memorial to commemorate what would have been her Jack's 47th birthday was unbearable.

Then the Warren report issued some findings, and they were different to what she recalled. That first shot had not, in fact, missed, but had hit both JFK and the Texas Governor who was riding in the car with them. The second shot had also hit its target, and only the third had gone wild.

And footage showed her crawling onto the back of the car (we now know to retrieve a part of her husband's skull) but she had no recollection of doing this.

Indeed, Jackie realized, as often as the event intruded into the day and her sleep, her recollections were confused, and not backed up by the Warren report findings.

She gave her own report to the enquiry at home. Once again, she had to revisit the event, and describe it. It was not the kind of rehabilitation the still mourning woman needed.

But understanding of the grieving process was poor back in the 1960s, and the advice she received from the Kennedys, from others around her and even from herself was that she needed to get a grip and move on.

Another source of her guilt was taking an extended, two and half week break to Europe following the death of Patrick. It had been with her sister, and they had stayed on the yacht of their friend, Aristotle Onassis.

On her return, Jack had tried to ease her out of her grief, and she had often snapped at him, although it was also one of the closest times of their marriage, brought together by grief.

'I had made an effort and succeeded, and he had really come to love me and to congratulate me on what I did for him. And then, just when we had it all settled, I had the rug pulled out from under me without any power to do anything about it,' she told Father McSorley.

What we know now is that Jackie was suffering from a form of post-traumatic stress disorder. Not only had her husband been taken away so publicly, but she had been as close a witness to the event as she could possibly be.

The British Prime Minister, Harold MacMillan, came closest to identifying the problem. As a war veteran, he too had suffered the impossible to define but still very real pain she was experiencing.

It was almost a year after the assassination that she took the decision that she had to move, along with the children, out of Washington, and purchased the New York apartment mentioned earlier.

What we know today, but did not back then, was that a change of environment offers no long-term solution.

Earlier, and during some of her worst times, Look magazine began to put together a special memorial issue for the President.

They wanted to print an upbeat story about how she had dealt with her loss, one that could not be further than the truth.

They wanted her to present as a stoic, bravely moving on while the children were getting over things with the support of their Uncle, Bobby.

Remember, the Kennedys always closed ranks in times of trouble. They were keen to support the articles.

The pressure told, and Jackie agreed to the story. The Kennedys then considered how best she could support Bobby's growing political aspirations further.

He launched a film about his brother, and wanted Jackie by his side, but she instead headed to Europe once again, leaving the children with her mother while she had a break.

In the end, she flew in just for the day of the film's launch, but could not manage all of the planned events. The film reopened the still festering wounds, and she went backwards once more.

The move to New York made things better. For just a day. With her children, she booked into a hotel while the apartment was redecorated.

They had a good time in Central Park, rowing on the lake, and were largely unrecognized. But the following day she agreed to pop into Bobby's campaign headquarters after dropping Caroline off at her new school.

She did so, with John Jr in tow. What she did not know was that campaign staff had alerted the press, and she left the building to be overwhelmed by crowds and journalists.

Once again, panic ensued. She adored her brother in law, but his ambition (like that of many of the Kennedy clan) usurped the needs of his brother's family.

The Warren report findings did not help either. Some comfort might have been gained had he died as a martyr for some great cause.

But those initial reports said that he had been the unfortunate victim of a lone, crazed gun man, killed without any real reason.

Like modern day sufferers of post-traumatic stress disorder, she began to fear things that had not occurred. The thought that one day a book called something like The Day the

President Was Assassinated filled her with dread.

She was terrified of the memories such a book might evoke, even though that one was not planned.

But many others were. She was already trying to distance herself from Manchester's authorized biography, fearful of the feelings it would invoke. But across the world, books were appearing; including one from Europe called 'Who Killed Kennedy?'

She tried to respond by re-contacting Manchester, telling him that he was the only official biographer.

But he felt that she wanted to dictate the content of his book, and was offended.

Life magazine published a report on the Warren Commission, a fellow journalist wrote a book, she had to get through the anniversary and a year on, the assassination was still all across the papers.

One task she had to complete was to sign off the design of her husband's grave. The architect of this, John Warnecke, would later claim that Jackie signed off the design and then went to bed with him.

She tried to mark the anniversary of the assassination as a turning point, and arranged for some public appearances after this date. But her condition could not be addressed as easily as this, and she was unable to honor her commitments.

Chapter Six – Moving On

Both during her marriage to JFK, and in the years after his death, Jackie have been rumored to have had many lovers.

The truth or otherwise of such claims is hard to know, with allegations of a liaison with bi sexual Russian ballet dancer Rudolf Nureyev harder to believe that talk of an illicit act with Bobby Kennedy, when both were in a state of emotional turmoil.

Nureyev is alleged to have complained, when drunk one night in London in the late sixties, that he has been involved with the former first lady for many years. He made similar claims regarding male members of the Kennedy family, as well as with Jackie's young sister, Lee Radziwill.

Stories abound, including that she had a romance with Marlon Brando and Italian car boss Gianni Agnelli, but seemed to be based on little more than photos taken of her with these friends which are as likely to be evidence of sharing a swim or time on the beach as of anything more sexual.

Nevertheless, Jackie was considered a style icon. Moreso prior to her husband's death, but still her dress sense was original and stylish.

By 1965 Jackie was showing some signs of coming to terms with her loss. Her children were growing up, and demanding a lot of her time, and she travelled regularly unveiling memorials to her husband, and promoting other Kennedy family members.

In May, 1965 the site where the Magna Carta has been signed seven hundred and fifty years previously saw the opening a British memorial to the assassinated president.

That charter had been an early guarantee of human rights, and it was therefore a fitting place for a tribute to a President who wanted to reform American politics.

In 1965, the Queen and Jackie Kennedy unveiled the memorial, which included a stone with words from the President's inaugural address engraved on it.

His two children were also in attendance. Fifty years later, the granddaughter he never met, Tatiana Schlossberg, laid a wreath of remembrance at the site.

Another use of Jackie's time during this difficult period was her work with the John F Kennedy Presidential Library and Museum.

Here is the repository for the official papers of the Kennedy administration. The building was designed by the architect I.M Pei, and is located in his family's original home town of Boston.

Of more concern was an event in 1966, when William Manchester's biography was finally ready for publication.

It contained details of JFK's private life that neither Jackie, nor the remainder of the Kennedy clan, wished to be known.

They sought to block the publication, which drew much media attention. They threatened to sue the publishers and finally came to a settlement whereby certain passages were removed.

Shortly after this, a long-time friendship blossomed into something a little stronger. Former British ambassador to the United States, and member of the aristocracy, David Ormsby Gore had been friends with the Kennedys for some time.

In 1967, his own wife was killed in a car accident, and Lord Harlech, as was his title and Jackie had something in common.

They toured Cambodia- these were the days when the war in Vietnam was at its height, and opposition in the US was growing ever stronger. They became known as the US's unofficial ambassadors to the region and were instrumental in repairing strained relations between the two countries.

For Ormsby Gore at least, the friendship grew much stronger than something purely platonic, and he proposed to the former first lady.

She turned him down, but wanted to remain close friends; she said that he reminded her too much of the days of marriage to JFK, and that ruled out any opportunity for marriage.

Another major event, to which she went, which also brought back bad memories, was the funeral of Martin Luther King, in Atlanta, Georgia in 1968.

The thought of the crowds had originally deterred her from attending, but her influence over the US people remained strong, and her presence was very important.

As we have alluded to, Jackie became very close to Bobby in the days and years following JFK's death.

Their relationship had always been close. He had spent time with her following her miscarriage, and she described him as the Kennedy least like his father.

For a while, he became like a surrogate father to the young children. For his part, he had felt guilt about his brother's assassination as we saw earlier, and credited Jackie for ensuring he stayed involved in politics.

By 1968, with opposition to the Vietnam War a major hindrance to the credibility of Lyndon Johnson. Robert Kennedy was persuaded to run for President on the Democratic ticket.

He, though, would only do so with Jackie's agreement. She was unsure, being worried about his safety. But she also felt that he should follow his beliefs.

Bobby felt he could do good, and despite his own worries about personal safety stood, and appeared as though he could even win the Presidency.

He was celebrating with friends following victory in the California Primary in June 1965 when he shot and fatally wounded.

Jackie flew immediately from her New York home to Los Angeles, and stayed by his bedside with his own family and wife, Ethel, but he never regained consciousness.

Many experts and others have claimed over the years that Jackie and Bobby shared more than a familial love.

But then again, people love a gossip, and some love to do down those they have put on a pedestal.

We will never know for sure, and really should believe that their relationship was proper throughout.

The death of Robert Kennedy reignited the depression Jackie suffered following the death of JFK. She became convinced that her connections to the Kennedy family made both her and her children targets.

She needed to get out of the country.

Chapter Seven - Jackie O

Jackie Kennedy had met Aristotle Onassis early in her marriage to JFK. Ari, as he was known to those close to him, had become a dear and valued friend to Jackie and it was only sometime after the assassination of her husband that romance began to grow.

Onassis had a wealth which even put that of the Kennedys in the shade, indeed he was one of the world's wealthiest men, a shipping magnate from Greece.

Their courtship evolved, and Ari could offer Jackie something that no one in America could, the confidence that she and her family were away from whatever threats the US offered.

There was a twenty-three-year age difference between the two, but that did not matter to Jackie.

Her wedding was held on Onassis's private island of Skorpios on October 20th, 1968 and her children held the candles typical of a Greek Orthodox wedding.

However, the move suddenly changed the perception of Jackie in America. Firstly, the Kennedys were going out of fashion, along with politics in general. Watergate was just around the corner, and Vietnam was changing the natural order of life.

Plus, the American public saw Jackie as one of their own, and there was a sense of betrayal felt by many when she took the decision to marry a European.

That she also changed her name (naturally enough, we may think today) to Jackie Onassis also caused consternation.

She began to receive negative media coverage in the US, where the perception that she and her family should foyer be victims held sway.

The change of name and marriage also meant that the secret service protection she had been receiving would end.

Although she retained her country horse farm and New York apartment (which had no less than fifteen rooms) she would now spend more and more time in her husband's various residencies around the world.

The media labelled her Jackie O, implying a fun-loving disregard for her responsibilities, although the security she now found for herself and especially her children should have been better understood in her homeland.

But for all this, her wedding was wonderful, with her close sister and close family members and friends attending the event.

Following the wedding, Jackie stayed close to the Kennedy family, often meeting with Ted, who would accompany her on public appearances.

But pressure mounted, and the press made claims that she would be ex-communicated from the Catholic Church, something Boston's Archbishop Cardinal Richard Cushing completely dismissed.

And with the paparazzi never far away, much time was spent on the shipping owner's enormous, 325 ft. yacht.

But on one occasion, before they were married but were much in love, a local journalist managed to get on board the luxury boat.

There an evening of drunken revelry took place, during which Onassis threw up several times. The journalist was a friend of one of the band members the billionaire had hired, and caught it all.

Ted Kennedy was also on board, organizing financial matters over the marriage, and allegedly he was presented with a blond escort for the night, although he was a married senator.

When it became apparent that the journalist was more than just a guest, Kennedy's security staff pressured the man, and he left, but on arriving back in Athens, he discovered that Onassis had also leant on the military junta leading Greece at that time.

All references to Kennedy were removed from the story. Perhaps evidence that there was a darker side to the Kennedys and

Onassis, if any such confirmations are needed.

In 1973, Ari's son was killed in a plane crash and the magnate never really recovered. He became ever more difficult, and fell into poor health.

The question as to the extent to which the marriage would survive this never arose, because in a Paris hospital in 1975 he died of pneumonia.

He was buried on his private island, and his estate was divided between his family and with Jackie receiving a smallish part of it.

In the space of a dozen years she had seen two husbands die.

Chapter Eight – Family Matters

Jackie's relationship with her sister, the American socialite Lee Radziwill, was (like many in her life) complicated.

That relationship was pushed to its limit by Jackie's marriage to Aristotle Onassis – he and Radziwill had been romantically involved with each other while Jackie Kennedy was in the White House with JFK.

In fact, it was Onassis who 'begged her to attend their wedding.' But Lee felt a sense of betrayal from her sister over the marriage, something from which the two never properly recovered.

It was notable that in her will, Jackie left keepsakes and mementos to many family members, including some to Lee's children. But she left nothing to her sister.

Both sisters had grown up close to their father, the roguish 'Black Jack' Bouvier. But Jackie was usually the successful one when the two were compared. She was the one who won at horse shows; she was the one who scored the top grades at school.

But the two were intensely close as children, perhaps enduring their parents' divorce and being thrust suddenly into a large, but welcoming, family when their mother remarried were factors behind this.

As young women, Lee was still in her late teens, the two sisters toured Europe in the summer of 1951, where the two young ladies had a whale of a time, sneaking into first class dinner dances on ships, and meeting icons of the art and culture world.

During her sister's time in the White House, those old childhood rivalries re-emerged. The sisters were still close, but Lee felt cast once again into the shadows, and also under extra attention simply for being sister to the First Lady.

Another cause of a minor niggle was that while everybody associated Jackie with the role of style icon, it was often her sister who advised her on what to wear.

But these are normal sibling rivalries – undoubtedly there were times when Jackie envied her sister for the additional privacy she was able to enjoy.

Living as a President's wife means being as much under the microscope of media and public attention as would face a member of the Royal Family.

In 1962, Jackie and Lee visited India and Pakistan together, on an official state visit. Again, while evidence that the two were close, for they were travelling together, some rivalry naturally emerged.

While Jackie received ovations and chants of welcome, Lee would sit still and silent next to her, receiving none of the same adoration.

But she equally understood that she was sitting next to the wife of the Leader of the Free World, a complex situation.

And it was around this time that speculation grew over Lee's relationship with Ari Onassis. The Greek was unpopular in the US, where he had been sued earlier, and was mistrusted by the Kennedys.

A headline of the time said: 'Does the ambitious Greek tycoon hope to become the brother in law of the American President?'

Then the family had the idea that Lee should accompany JFK on an extended tour to Europe. Jackie was heavily pregnant at the time, and unable to travel.

Lee loved the experience, and for a while it brought the two sisters even closer to each other.

That pregnancy ended badly, with the boy, Patrick, surviving for only three days. Jackie had the comfort of Lee flying in to be at her bedside, and later the two flew out to join Onassis on his yacht.

Perhaps the seeds of the later marriage were laid at this event. For his part, Onassis largely stayed out of the way, working in his state rooms, and leaving the sisters to their own company.

But on parting, both were given gifts, with Jackie's diamond and ruby necklace outscoring the tiny bracelets he gave to Lee.

Yet more reason for jealousy.

But Lee was still loyal to her sister. When JFK was assassinated, she spent much time with Jackie and the children. But for all this, the strain of Jackie's depression began to tell on her.

'She's really more than half round the bend! She can't sleep at night and she can't stop thinking about herself and never feeling anything but sorry for herself,' she said to a close friend during one particularly stressful time.

Jackie's mixed up mental state even led her to slap her sister on one occasion, such was her inability to cope with the fact that Lee was still married, while she was widowed.

As tragic as it was, in some strange ways JFK's death was liberating for Lee. She was no longer sister in law to the US President, and she had more privacy and freedom to do as she wished.

In the seventies, Lee and Jackie reconciled their differences, and worked together on a documentary about their former home which had fallen into disrepair, and was being lived in by an aunt.

They restored the house, although once again it was Jackie who got most of the glory.

That was really the story of their relationship; never fully falling out, but always something present to be a hindrance, be it sibling jealousy or a US President.

Perhaps not an unusual tale of a sibling relationship.

John Jr Kennedy, Jackie and JFK's youngest child hardly knew his father, being just three years old when the President was assassinated. But he shared with him an early and untoward death.

He had been the first ever child born to a President elect, his birth coming between the election and his father's inauguration.

He travelled with his mother in the intervening years between her marriages, and the two were intensely close. But John Jr never warmed to his stepfather, considering Ari Onassis a bit of a joke.

That his mother's love towards her second husband cooled quickly might have been a reason for this.

John Jr was a keen pilot, and was flying his family in their plane when it crashed into the sea off of Martha's Vineyard, and all on board were killed.

John's older sister is the last surviving member of the nuclear family who lived in the White House in the early sixties.

She is today an author and diplomat, having been the US ambassador to Japan until 2017. She is also an attorney.

Caroline Kennedy was very close to both her mother and her brother. Another significant person in the children's lives was their nanny Maud Shaw.

But for all the pressures on her time, Jackie was very much a hands-on mother. She loved to read them stories, and they would spend many hours painting together.

For Jackie, despite her own advantages growing up, and the luxuries the White House offered, she wanted the children to be brought up in a humble way.

They would, for example, have to pick up their own dirty clothing, and although surrounded by secret service agents, the children were forbidden to use them as servants.

Good manners were instilled from a young age, and the children were encouraged to mix with youngsters from all walks of life, as well as the extended Kennedy clan.

They would, for example, go with their nanny or Jackie to the local part, and play with local friends.

Those in the White House during those early years of the children's lives tell that it was Jackie who handled the discipline, often making the naughtier John Jr stand in the corner to find his manners.

But she was also fun and playful with her children. She loved running and chasing them on the lawn. And she spent many hours teaching young Caroline to ride.

One incident that personified that particular closeness came in 1962 when Jackie was teaching Caroline how to water ski. To do this she simply put her young daughter in front of her on the single set of skis.

Some of the press was up in arms, feeling it was dangerous for the young child, but Jackie just laughed.

When their father was killed, a rift occurred between the beloved Maud and Jackie. At their grandmother's insistence, it was Maud who told Caroline that her father had been killed.

It was, of course, a job the mum felt she had to do herself.

Jackie then, as we saw earlier, fell into a decline, and felt that she was letting down her children. Those close to her, though, felt that she was still doing a good job, keeping things as normal for the youngsters as was possible.

She took them later on a long pilgrimage to Ireland, to see their ancestral land and it was fear for their safety after Bobby Kennedy's death that persuaded Jackie to move the family from the US.

Chapter Nine – Jackie's Later Years

After the death of Aristotle Onassis, Jackie started a career in publishing. Her friend, the Viking Press president, Thomas Guinzburg, offered her a role as a consulting editor.

The stayed in this position for a couple of years, but fell out when a Jeffrey Archer novel about a plot to assassinate a President, a younger Kennedy, was published by the firm.

It was too close to home.

In 1978, becoming more and more private, she took a job with an old friend, Nancy Tuckerman who had been her social secretary in her White House days. This too was in publishing.

Jackie was not in any way becoming reclusive, but she was enjoying being away from public attention.

She would spend her social time with her children, and some years later, her grandchildren. She would still attend social events, but not as often. Jackie was working for three days a week, getting through a dozen books per year, and also taking long holidays to Martha's Vineyard.

Those who worked with her in those days speak highly of her. Those values of determination and hard she had instilled in her children were evident in her editing, which was kindly but thorough.

Her adoration for the books she edited was apparent, and she had a great ability to see through frauds and get to the heart of people she met.

She also enjoyed the fact that she was working out of the limelight. She highlighted that in publishing, the editor gets little glory, and that was something that she liked.

While she did not marry, she forged a very close relationship with a Belgian born diamond merchant and industrialist.

Maurice Templesman was a frequent companion to her, and they would holiday together in her Martha's Vineyard mansion.

In 1982 he moved in with her full time, and their relationship was confirmed to friends and family. But by now, interest in Jackie Kennedy was on wane, and she was able to enjoy a good deal of privacy with this, the last man who would share her life.

Jackie still mixed with the political elite. She was still a part of the Kennedy family. She and Maurice were particularly close to the Clintons, hosting them for dinners and spending time on Maurice's yacht with them.

Jackie also became very interested in American landmarks and worked hard to help to preserve them.

As she entered later middle age, Jackie remained fit. She and Maurice would enjoy a stroll through Central Park, and she was a regular jogger.

She loved playing with her grandchildren, and kept her healthy looks.

It was therefore a particular surprise when, at the age of sixty-three, she was diagnosed with non-Hodgkin's lymphoma, a particular virulent and hard to cure cancer.

Jackie immediately underwent chemotherapy and other treatments, and was able to continue to work in her book editing role for a while.

She maintained as near a normal life as possible, still honoring her social commitments, and spending as much time with her family as she could.

But her condition worsened quickly. She entered the New York Cornell Medical Centre in the middle of May, 1994, just four months after her initial diagnosis.

But she left two days later, with the hospital able to do little more.

She died on the 19th May, with Maurice and her family at her bedside.

She was just 64 years old.

But although those last years of her life were the quietest, the least glamorous and the least public of her full but short life, they were, we can hope, the best.

With a man she loved, who was completely faithful to her, with two children of whom she was proud, working hard and with some degree of privacy, she found peace.

Conclusion

How is Jackie Kennedy remembered today, more than fifty years after the blood soaked pink dress created an image that seared the minds of the world?

Firstly, despite her short fall from popularity during the 'Jackie O' years, she is still perhaps the most popular first lady of all time.

A young mum and committed wife to a still popular president. Somebody who fulfilled her duties while never neglecting her own children.

Her style, grace and dress sense still inspire. As a traveler, she embraced different cultures and helped to breed tolerance in a world as ravaged by war today as it was in the late 1960s.

Her love of art or historic monuments and of literature has helped to preserve many important artefacts and buildings.

Indeed, the White House today is as it is largely because of her interventions.

Jackie Kennedy led a glamourous - at times tough, at times happy, at times challenging - life.

But we can say that she lived it to the full.

35846157R00139